THE DOTTERY

PITT POETRY SERIES
ED OCHESTER, EDITOR

THE DOTTERY

KIRSTEN KASCHOCK

UNIVERSITY OF PITTSBURGH PRESS

Published by the University of Pittsburgh Press, Pittsburgh, Pa., 15260
Manufactured in the United States of America
Printed on acid-free paper
10 9 8 7 6 5 4 3 2 1
ISBN 13: 978-0-8229-6319-6
ISBN 10: 0-8229-6319-1

This book is the winner of the 2013 Donald Hall Prize in Poetry, awarded by the Association of Writers and Writing Programs (AWP). AWP, a national organization serving more than three hundred colleges and universities, has its headquarters at George Mason University, Mail Stop 1E3, Fairfax, VA 22030.

The Donald Hall Prize for Poetry is made possible by the generous support of Amazon.com.

four—my buoys—who for each blessing drag me up

If we start by postulating the essential sameness . . . we shall learn no more about that sameness.

Susanne K. Langer

CONTENTS

It is essential to note that manifestoes, their tiny toes, are generally written to defend the birth of the monster rather than messily during conception. They are not, therefore, prior acts and should not be admitted into the building, usually a hospital, but sometimes a place with an altar where, if castrati were present, which they never fully are, they would refuse song because it, like most art, is beautifully a reason for mutilation.

I.

WOUND

Matter is merely a storeroom.

—Wassily Kandinsky

The first dottery was called Limbo.

Before the first dottery was shut down it had twenty million legs across the steppes. It was like a thaw. It meant itself too, almost exclusively. Before it was eliminated, consigned to the once-drawer, the curio-city, Limbo was overdant—so lush with the unspoken it pirouetted on its own face, on the rolling buttocks of its own hills. It was a plague of giraffes, chewing trees, preventing oxygen. Beatific. Before it was sent to your room, where it waits still, in ancient meditation on bedframe, the first dottery was a vibrant bully—out storking the streets and prairies for the godless, ready to swoop in like the end times and carry off our weakest.

Which leads me to my question for our current dottery: What are we to do with our weakest? Who will own them?

A bone spider wove it out of brick. The bricks came out her ass like silk constipation. The mortar, threads between. This was the original secretion. No one still knows where the dottery suspends. Each new dew and it is gone from yesterday's span across the grass. The dottery houses women before they are conceived. The building teaches them waiting. The walls teach confinement. The inner warden teaches them how to occupy their small time with things that fit in hand. One-window teaches them the moon. The dotters learn it all so that it seems familiar when it is taught again or else they are bored abhorrent and so unlearn. Dotters know this: all things undone contain their enemies. Dotters are not dotters from anatomy, dotters are dotters from edits, diets, tides, the cakey residue of Desitin in folds of infinite orchid. They arrive in silk, flee down ropes of root.

The failure I began with was the failure to be brilliant.
Fables have a remarkable habit of transparency.

You're no star—my sister has told me.
I see, I say. I, eye, sir.

I am much brighter (true-bling) than you are, unless you are reading this
my book of prosies (one potato, two potato)—

these unbirthdays all mine—and deriving
some proof.

WARNINGS: Some orphanages happen before birth—preconceptions herein are mobbish, little more than unruly tenets. Evict. Some orphanages are theaters with no stage to ovate toward, no postpartum afterproduction, no violent, satisfying striking of the set. Some orphanages are nail salons where patrons are taught, like children, manicures cancer. But manicures don't.

Artery-red, the dottery is a brickbox warehoused near the next street over. Schoolroom-style, very like a church, it migrates every other day to its present location. It is a piggy-bank, and you can make a deposit through the mail slot. A pale pink embryo. Hers are left all the time. All the time develops hers into dottage—the substance of the boutique. Also, clothes can be left. Catholic plaids, Swiss dots, thigh-highs, shantung. Inside the dottery, dotters are fashioned—matched to apparel.* You asked. This is how.

> How should a dotter go? With god.
> How should a dotter live? Against given.
> How should a dotter be? Trou-bling.
> How should a dotter care? Church her.
> How should I treat a dotter? Sugar.

---

* Engendering: the putting on, or in, of the first undergarment. Planted unmentionably, painsgivingly, beneath skin with skewers or very straight razors, it is not unlike botfly larva, as it can appear to have arrived beforehand and from another country.

A dotter is pre-ironic, a bored vessel.
A dotter leaks.

A dotter mislays, misdirects, misogynies, misses America, mistakes
me for someone.

A plot may be narrower, in the torso, than a child's grave.
A child's life is a lie told often enough.

We are talking ideas. Ideas take up very little space
inside. Inside ideas are dark and dry.

Mistletoes, the tiny tiny toes.
A dotter is not a tattoo.

In once-upon-time, dotters were promised a world of frosting. Whitespun and brittle and dissolving in the tongue cupped to the roof of the mouth. Chewing they were instructed to understand as unnecessary, nor allowed. Teeth were designed explicitly for display. No one told the ramifications of sugar: the abscess and rush—the moral decay. Sugar was to those original dotters a grazing field for yeast. An addiction bed, an affair, a fling. Still, they loved it even as it proved itself shallow and brief—afterward, the very air bitter. Dotters have been regularly educated to their detriment. Sugar is often their fondest wish. It is why some agree to be born, and how they would die.

: nevertheless, a manifesto

1. Dotters are not usurpers of the solar but its eclipsing. The sun, since banging out, has been unworthy of the direct gaze. Not so with dotters. Dotters have known much gaze and are equipped to array it prismatically. To spatter it.

2. Dotters do not connect, do not scribble midafternoon manifestoes in midafternoon manifesto booklets. Instead, dotters seek, by their incomplete shun and elliptical hides, to scalp the lyrical I— to remove the hair and the chocolate from the blonde and say: "See, a bleeding woman on a horse—she's got—what brains!"

3. Dotters fall down.

4. Dotters are interested in pastoral only as a way to fetish. You like streams? Babel not, cum in one.

5. Dotters chill barons. They deliver. The barons have ever feared dotters because of the ice. The beds of cold.

6. Dotters are not semisweet surrealists. They are hard cookies. They don't want to nudge you to a slightly uncomfortable spot. They'd rather break your teeth, but oh so obliquely.

7. Dotters are by definition one-dimensional, one-trick ponies, specks. *You* think.

8. Enough dotters, taken together, form a second-type story—a curvy hyperbolic form. Staircase, sex, a helix bound by sugars.

9. Dotters evolved sporadically, from the space between forage and pillage. Between gore and will.

10. Dotters are to foster confessional sci-fi wherever it is found. As a sister-craft, a dovecote.

11. If you wish to be a dotter, buy your tickets for the dottery now. There is currently a sacrifice. There is always currently a sacrifice.

12. Dotters, to be fair, are forever opening and closing the curtains. Doing a peepshow disguised as aubade. The difference between the two is address. A black dress, the kind brides wear.

2.

DUAL

Sometimes it is necessary to make a confrontation—and I like that.

—Louise Bourgeois

I was a dotter on the field. I was wind. I ground my teeth and took the buoys down by their chains. Shark, I careened beneath grass or under woodchips surrounding equipment. I adored equipment. Net, bars, anything jailish. Missiles too. What dotter doesn't love a thrown thing? Fight. Kiss. Gauntlet. On the field a dotter can work the war, other than to sew or whore. Can take the furies usually pled out through fingertips and torso them, or limb them all to hell. On the field was where I met my holies. My Jack, my Charlie, my Mark, my Jane. Together we gamed as if the sun were everyone's. We took our meat and set it to letters. We scrabbled our bodies quartz, zephyr, axial. We scrabbled our bodies zygote. (It was never every tile.) Later. After. The field folds down in a sudden mudslide. My wind is swallowed up. I don't know direction. I don't know where, really, wrong went.

The failure to risk is not the failure I want today to bear.
The aggression part I am I am just now learning to reinhabit.

Most angry at most of the time: me—
for letting them think it's over, spinning wheels

so sleepy beauts can-can continue sleep. I loom
to cover no freezing, clothing only my own astounding

nakedness in the fashion of language
which is fashion.

I'm learning the disease word (communicate) and to say—time.
You and I should by now be naked and more than a century grown.

The designation "dotter" illustrates a certain unspelunked specificity: one's identity finds no twin in cross-stitching, scarification, tattoo, or piercing in relief. Preliminarily mapped, a dotter is all limitation and railing, as is the nature of preliminary maps. What you want to realize is that several colors busted as they brought her edge about. Starboard. She is a wax precipice—in that, drawn, the dimensions drop deeply away, unbuttressing her. Leaving her susceptible to light. Her blinding, fourth-dimensional parts are etched, roughed, into limestone cloud. She is left, but condensed or desiccated—at any rate—more artful. Cathedraled. Dotter is a cutout, a flay. A pair of mimes out of papier-mâché, the last Matisse. She is de rigueur, but up in her crow—actual fathoms below actual cave floor—and not to sail. Moby this. Moby that.

It is required we adopt all slurs now, like purse-fed Pomeranians. But what if I do not feel like a pussy, not for dinner, or if cunt has too many teeth or none (all guy-smiley muppet-mouthed)? What if I cannot even wrap legs or lips, upper nor nether, around grrl? And what if I consider myself, yoga, very flexible? To think I used to dance. Tables, drunk, heads of pins. Something has come to be stodged in my policy. I long to flicker television-like on no prehistoric wall, vine legs round no patriotic pole, nor flagrantly flower in some suburban bed only to be put out like cigarette.

To talk talk.
I need to use it to speak to you but can twist it is myth.

The confederate flag is not not about slavery for Athenians who wish it
    as they wish Meemaw had not shown up in her best Sunday best
    for lynchings.
My ancestors were rapists.

I recognize control is not inside my mouth—no I know now means yes.
Still, when I hear how bitch Hillary is, it is not how I wished to say
    the word.

Except to my college roommate
that one, that one time.

You were the favorite. This, at the wedding, her a matron, a mutter-er, ushered down to her minimum, an aged baroque. She was not heavy, this was not strip-mining, and there was more. We loved you glued. We loved you corseted. We loved you hooved and harangued and lacking gloves. It was not her glory that was now for sale. Shamed, she would have let it go at basement. Because. Look what you have not done. Have not made. Lined up tall to short since homecoming—things pinned coming after things bled dry. Well, this was to be expected. But. Where are your shoes? Your match-ing? Your duplication strategies? Where is your her? She was by the end blinking. Tail-lit. A car accident, mangle and windshield and sunglass. This was not her matinee. These were not her ovaries. She willed a bump to black. Went up in sacrifice to startle the catwalk. Sandbagged sweetly in a gobo—a ferny one. The cyc was blue.

18

The failure to be relevant to whom.
Write no seek no teach no one.

Underestimate no intellect of no reader, dilute no
message. Don't have messages.

Redundancy is distasteful except in Stein.
Box, and box and a tongue inside.

There be no I in me, no mean author, both dead
at least terribly and so forth on the inside.

From the body is lately a souvenir
of womanhood—its terrible insides.

The way poetry's treated by other poets: as theirs, and thus
susceptible to dogmas themselves reactions to other dogmas.

You and I are not a dogma
person.

I was taught all about stolen. Stolen was mine own: words, ore, hours,* breath. Everything was to be borrowed for me, and I would never be allowed to return anything because of the stain. My imprint was not a mark of worth. Surface was. To gloss. I was taught to beget myself postmodernly, produce likenesses, and then found I could not. I refused it, but barely, began to hear the chime and cantor in the word *essence*, although I knew it was wrong to feel an underneath, beneath the photograph, the bone, that bit of world I need to suck. Absent nipple. Scattersource. Where the bees have bored, there bore I. Our flute our hollow fibula our flower—the bees. Mine.

---

* To recapture, directions say—grow younger. Kill. Birth. Apply moisturizer. Be convertible, as in car not sofa. Bankrob, bancroft, botox. Be the belle. Bag the bling. You can-can never be too wretched thing.

20

Dotters con you in mystical grift. You came from the dottery, to the dottery you will return. Egged on, spoonfed. Once oh once oh, you sing, I was a dotter. True. Like buckwheat is true, like twinkie. In Candida I renounced them. I resigned from dot, daught, doubt, debt—from all monies. I became an excommunique. A click. The sterile guns fired. The billboard read—She Is a Gift—Only Eighteen Installments. The car feigned sleep on the overpass so as to lose the heist. I never reentered my passwords. I never saw a need.

Has a dotter. She nextdoor does. Some nextdoor do. (Jealousy and criticism are french kissers—to prepare this photograph: saw the face of the corpse in half but leave it attached at the tongue.) Unlike some, it is not a disease, a dotter. It is not by proxy. Diabetic. She is in the bed with her. It is natural, a symbol of love. To be in the bed. Some distrust this way with the dotter. Foreign-hand. Dropsy. Dottering on the lea. These some, they are outside. Hurt you, Mummy. Hurt you. To the buoys you say, just, just the ones talking trash. Away the big conundrums. Mummy will rhythm or raven the outside from you. Meanwhile, a mummy raises in vigilance, beats the keep. You say, no hurt. Nun. But to a dotter all lies are told on or below the level of bone. The way the infant is held. Restrained aversion. Some casual fingernails only, skin so like invitation. Better for a mutter to show her how hurt is dealt with, and after awhile— maintained.

The failure to recognize patterns is not a failure of imagination—
it is a wall incrementally smashed through with face.

Hatred is
and so damned filling.

Distrust all sate or shoot.
The no-remedy between is impotent, academic—not possible on a front.

I am dry inside because of especially the wet I distrust.
Color wet like paint, gender wet with esses, religion a damp lollipop.

Sugar is offered up—to every next molester—in slippery baton.
Prettyplease drop it, poppet.

What instead? Safety? Little-usions and ass-play in the claim of
        performing resistance?
I will not eat that, get in, help you look for your cat.

I had forgotten that part—how we'd been laundried—hung out. The wet clean part did not excruciate, but then the sun would go and the whipping begin. Not froth, domination. Would we be taken in, or end as the wet unclean? There were no safety words on the line. I wanted to pinch the clothespins from my clavicles, the little homunculi, and dig their two legs into the earth. An insert. It would feel good to, for once, punish. And there were the blessings, buoys, dipping in and out of our rows, our sails before storms, braving the involuntary red of our flap-and-thrash to seek what they sensed was hidden.

Satisfaction with one's backyard masquerades as wisdom, then stagnation. Inability to access any satisfaction at any time is a design flaw or someone sometime, your self or aunt, has sewn or stopped you up. The pipes. The dottery's architecture is in this way that of a large snowflake out of PVC: there are an endless array of angles, most awkward but prettily arranged, and some are leaking poison, self-loathing which makes its porcelain way to a center continually voided—in an act of self-loathing. But it is the brain I would target. Red stitched on the skull, a concentric cap and trade. How is she inscribed in the labyrinth? Is it? Possible then to redraw, retool, coax the Minotaur back for disembowelment, de-Daedalus? The red thread pulled as if upward through a cervix. This I would know: how I am made. Sewn? Printed? Digitized? Hewn from stone? Coagulated? Am I a calculation, a piece of pottery, a choreography of copper wire—welded into forever nursery? Can it be undone? Which art are thou? Art I? And what made me—dread godhand or meme or viral joke? Why don't I desire bloodsport, defend rhetorically torture, let water pass standing, command? It must be one: defect, salvation. Also: why happier in the questions? Why softer in the bed?

3.

TRIAGE

. . . there's a difference to be told.

—Bernadette Mayer

Entering the dottery, slipped: a threshold creased with lard. From your ass, the dotters lining the walls looked less like cringing. So many unached fors. Aborted ones of porcelain. Daffodillings. Tin-roofed and footed ones and straw others and ones of brickshit. *If, if, if I had a square ass.* A grandmutter quipped through the building. Engine. Dotters do not want chosen. They want ungotten, dropped into batter for later expansion—to be needful, doubled in earnest. But from ass-on-threshold, the dottery seemed not rhapsodic, rather a school with room for the willing. All the dotters could poltergeist. They were all too fourteen. You might have asked one to cohabit, offered a lavender glove. But to be getting any from here was unwholesome—though not completely unlike twisting a skull from between your own legs. Ah. Blood brown. Fine. Fetal.

The failure to rise above.
I have made it my business—the counting of vaginas (one potato two).

Lately, it's been more of a hobby.
How many where earning what for what. What for what.

When I come to a room with too few vaginas, I have a long knife for
    opening some up.
In faces or along the bikini line (although more discreet, there is of
    course to deal with the intestinal matter).

Wandering into the wilds of too many—
elementaries, nursing homes, malls, ballet class, waitresses—I also
    long to.

Open one up. Up Poppinslike this time, either for flying
or for keeping sleet off me daisy.

Dotter freezes in the julep. She is terrifyingly mint. You coined her name for a poem and now you're done in. Tucked. Dotter was the space you reserved for avalanche. All the white in a blast, all the ways to lost. If you would just accept a patron, all a king meant was you shouldn't put together things thrown down. Or impale, turn gaunt, and run. The Ming—a vessel—has been crazied, unglued, but isn't asked to hold water so won't dribble. That's infant, the series. You should say daily dotters instead of a single firm nation. Remember, it is our boundaries that keep us wholesale. And don't neglect the white horse dream that in your family is a death. Finally, at king's constant, mild urging: you outgun the unborn. It is to be your new hobby.

Why is it you're the mourning? Is it the impasse, the mountain you can't one afternoon cross? An intersection locked. They, the loved ones you, the ones you've been allowed, walk North/South: attention to heat. You—held to latitude by a lower field of gravity—hurt. It isn't a real city, real map, building, door, rope, bridge, bleeder. You are not accountable to molecules: their knowable weights, configurations, orbits, enzymes, times of day. Someday something will serve as a catalyst. A dotter can wait. A table. Or a brick wall. And so. What? Accuse me of something. I can hear you under this caterwaul, this dispelled gospel tract as it has been in through the mudroom, heart. I listen to the way you are, hymn of you, so quiet when I am talking of them, them not mine. Just say I shouldn't. That it is enough. Tell me what it is I'm missing in these boxes, this attic of fucked.

How dare you want.
How dare I.

The factual inscape is that great poetry is not written by mutters,
   mutterers.
Women have said this. You seclude yourself: not everyone has
   experienced birth, for example.

Hearing them—I have failed to respond.
For this, as for all comas (snowingwhite, sleepy-beaut, schiavo), I
   am thought mute, or else as good a thing as dead.

The doll is not what the doll replaces. The doll is not what the thing the doll replaces was made to replace. The doll is not the roadtrip. The doll is not the pointe shoe. The doll is not the boyfriend. The doll is not the boyfriend's sister. The doll is not the mother or the sober. The doll has two spiderlashed black blinkable eyes. The doll has been pulled apart a thousand times for horror. The head of the doll on the side of the road at the edge of the surf will not watch you back. N'accuse. The doll cannot, in this way, be the subject of mutilation. The subject of mutilation is what you are after, but you must remember it is not the doll. The doll is what every dotter has been fashioned after, save her unfortunate insides.

In the soft-core snuff-ballet, "I'm Erica," there are no pointe shoes and no poor. In "I'm Erica," no one has had the abortions no one has admitted to having. In "I'm Erica," Canada is living above the garage. In "I'm Erica," California has left her abusive boyfriend for the second time, but she'll be back. In "I'm Erica," children do not go outdoors without precautions. A single parent. A bible. A halter-top. A handgun. "I'm Erica" and am post-wave. Forget hand-hand-wrist-wrist-wrist—I can prefer a hummer to the rose parade. I'm Erica, and I'm an alcoholic. I'm Erica and I do not hate women because I still fuck them, don't I? I do.

The failure of excess to exceed wants a response that thinks: a joke.
Perhaps about the dedicated ceramics, a bowl-shaped inversion of face
    so ulti-feminate, ex-tra-la-la-crescent, so moon.

To put it another way—a way acknowledging excess's physical and wet
    manifestation (so much sibilance, many esses)—

            porcelain faces are properly
            feces immune, if one uses
            a simple cloth

Q: Excess is continually aiming to exceed its own transgressions into
    what space?
A: Tile floor.
            ha-ha-ha-whore
                            chamber
    toilet,   pot :)

The inner warden examined their expenditures. You can't leave here without knowing things. I won't match you to a mutter. You'll end here, preconceived. She was brutal in the way they had been led to expect. Whores to what her. You can't hope to leave here without knowing things, she said it again. Thing one is: you can't hope at all, and although it's in you, it's wrong that it is. Like ovaries. Like the glitter we used to confetti through your oatmeal in a failed attempt at mass appeal. It's the things inside you make you stray. Scrape, scrape—but as you scrape—blow empty space into yourself, be flatable. Make your vapidity concrete. If you ask me, she said, rather than actual—you should seek to be life-sized. It's my job, you know: prophylaxis. I'm to keep you from yourselves, them from you, you from them. I'm supposed to condom you until you can yourselves. Tuck the portable halo of me deep inside your purse, half a hand-cuff, the whole of a dry well. If you leave here smart, I won't be used. Instead, you'll assume anyone-wants-you is diseased. It's safer, even. To abstain, self-loave. Sliced, white collapses and greens. The whole thing, she said, is very like—*very like*—spring.

It's a wonderful wife. The new year is a sigh. The inner warden opens the floor and swimming pool. Green or blue, but not in color. They take a naked dip at midnight and call it tobacco. Inside the water, the flesh they will repeatedly try to own is reminded of its content. A dotter is a series of membranes. A congregation of seals. Rings around the water: water, only domesticated. One of the dotters chooses her wet name. Some mutter will come for her tomorrow and, muttering, rename her dry. Once renamed, she will be clothed—a tankini perhaps, a single ruffle not quite over the ass, something appropriate. It is, all of it, in the ledgers. But for one hour of one night she will float with the others autonomous. There is a depth of nostalgia here unknown outside the dottery, a missing of some frivolous center. She chooses. Later someone may lasso her, the moon. Or ride her. Or hide her, robe, in a bush. But beyond piano, petals, beyond broken banister, she has not been the always and steadfast marry. If you take the time, or can replay it altered, pull your head out of your suicide and try whispering it. *Marzipan.*

Outside of the dottery—a half-rapture. Adrift like low zeppelins above their clothes. The brick facade of the dottery casts them as cartoon. Body bags, balloons. Text. Not yet lifted all the way up because of something-they. Maybe they-crewel. Maybe they-wrung-out-they-engagements or they-stringy-stringy-necks. The dotters face out the one-window. It is frowning. It is in a dotter's consonants to doubt, to skeptacle. Some of the two dozen floaters had left the dottery without buying, not asking even prices, not even pinching cheeks. Was this bankrupt? While the dotters performed both the watching and as barbarians, the almost-mutters rose and hung, their once-privates purpling in useless apartment. One of the dotters had a thought: *so this is it—a base display of our betters.* In other words, a reason for evolution.

One dotter was conceived a man. No, two. Twelve. Admission: there were hundreds. Thousands of men were not, priorly. Thousands of men pre-embryo could thread a needle with an eyelash, feel. Some retained water. Some were retrained. Some small rain down shall rain. The sum of their parts was not eagle to the hole-in-one. The hole *was* the part. Later, wholes were defined as solar—a system of orbits focused, buckets of electrons or planets swung around the largest tumor, largest mass, that ritual taking up of most. It is after all, after everything, space and weight and not the scarlet robes or scepters, clubs, and balls that makeup power. A dotter should learn from this not to mince her steps. Instead, flesh out and out and out.

During a periodic upwelling of the dottery: "We must sever. The umbilici, the ledgers, all cordage torched. As utterances out of mutters' mouths we cannot originate. We must end this and never rise. Refuse to be strung up as kites or heretics. We stay. Enseige ourselves. Cauterize. Since muttering is useless and awful—we must choose mutterlessness." Her inflammatories were met with rallying cries from the pelvic regions of the dottery. They centered their gravity by scraping the tips of all their matchsticks into all their blood. Then, an odd dotter who had mathematics and seizures spoke from a dark corner of her face. She had been hemming around the edges of the crowd, darts lost. But she was in agreement: "Those who carry us would re-selve our books as reference. I don't know you, but I won't atlas." "It's true," another yelled, "even the best fashion us, rubbing our ballets until we coo and please." And so they agreed for a time not to be had. They hatched a plan—to walk out on the dottery. They thought if they moved in that way out into the world, un-muttered, they would eventually turn, like milk, into something that could bear—instead of more of the same—a resemblance to solid.

4.

FEAR

They were minor deities; no temples were built to them.

—Jorge Luis Borges

played the clarinet. It was so musical, and there was the whole open mouth thing, the stroking of the reed with the flat of the tongue, the gentle bites that nudged the pliable wood into correct contact with the mouthpiece. She liked especially the upper register. She liked it bird-in-the-tree rather than bird-in-the-water. It mattered to her that the rhythms written for the clarinet were substantively different than the rhythms written for flute or for oboe. She did not yearn to be elsewhere. The syncopation, she felt, though autumn, was so tip of the tongue, so candy. Her love of the darker, percussive quality was a barely waking want inside her, and it pushed her, vaguely, from the classical, at least the most classical classical, into the bare peripheries of jazz, smoke and turkey and a certain wild, cool writhing on her stool though still long-skirted and crisp-bloused, until one late night, 3 maybe 4 a.m., robins even, she found its screech and its hammer—her pound of wail—the release into the narrow black bird that sent her through her fingers to its throat like the best, best murder.

so hated shrapnel. The way it got all through, the way it was said to infect. Shrapnel's dotter had become a physician's assistant because of her mediocre MCATs, because support from the family was lackluster. She could do nearly all a physician could do, which irritated her when she was waiting to get prescriptions signed by Dr. Freed talking on his cell to his wife. Apparently, there was algae in the pool filter. Shrapnel's dotter did okay, no Lexus, no Prada, some nightly Skyy. Okay. She had an expensive bird, didn't bother teaching it to talk. It was very green. Her hatred of shrapnel was theoretical. She never saw shrapnel in her practice. Just got lucky, she supposed, if a general lack of exploding things in her vicinity could be considered luck. Maybe if she had had to face it, she would have grown to appreciate and fear its tenacity. If she had been forced to tweeze it from some nasty maybe even gangrenous wounds, things might have turned out otherwise, but she was a PA in a very small town. A very nice, very small town, where no one saw much shrapnel until the day she detonated herself in the parking lot of the SuperWalMart.

They said of her later that she had been good with children, knew just how to distract them, and that they trusted her.

the dotters of Men

were more like dotters than sons. Were more yes than no. More snappish than pliant, more shoulders than knees. Wore more wool than silk. The dotters of Men had more fire than flint, more creole than pigeon, sauce than sugar. They roughened more than smoothened, shat more than squealed, tossed about more often than welled up at the corners. They wore themselves threadbare before having themselves replaced. The newer models they knew to be flimsier, a thin yogurt, with less architectural interest. Each of these dotters preferred her brick exposed. They were not incorruptible, however, and some spooned superciliousness into their tea. And some of these some preferred blow, because of even more. The dotters of Men could shoot up and steal and profit from the furs. They found little distasteful, and less not to their liking. They liked a lot. They loved. Hard, fast, in midair. A plummeting. They lived among men as if men were no different. In this way, they were taken in, a naive piecework, stray, a sharp breath indrawn at the peak. In this way, the dotters of Men founded a movement. It, too, was a plummeting.

diamond-minded—ate water and win-
nowed. Her fever was sharps. A way
had to be found for each secret to be
carried through. Pearls are coated. Not
that. She would not make pretty waste.
A tidy idea, her finite, she minted to its
last detail. She knew how diamonds
grew, bowelled in the earth for an age—
hers was to create a minute version in
modest frame. The key: condensation,
the pressing and diminishment, a pure
trail through a tight system.

She froze all her drink and chipped it
into fractions. Like amounts of rice
were bathed in heated almond oil until
translucent. She corseted a twelve-inch
waist. All rites were timed. The meting
out grain by grain of clear food wight-
ed her. Diet and whalebone tied her to
a room—too essential to run stairs of
castle, sweep floors of hovel.

Painstakingly disengaged from cir-
cumstance. And how refined.

She would not be outcome; she was a
maker. An entire life caged mattered
little if diamonds. All existence binds a
body—this she knew—her genius was

49

to increase constraint, not feint from.
Snake from lizard: she would be mind.
And mind unhindered by or breaking
flesh is diamond. The Achemist's dotter
went under with a sharp spoon. Along
the vein. The chips were in. She would
catch all in a let of blood—distillery.

O to have bled an end, a gem. Said
when.

took in all the Exorcist brought home:
smoke in brown bottles, fetal wisps
coiled around rosary beads, vapors
trailed from loafer heels. She scraped
it all into an antique copper tub for
bathing but saved that bath. It swirled
and foamed—the misshapen gas—it
lurched impolitely. It hissed. When,
out in the woodshed, she spoke
softly or crooned or read to it, when
she hummed or whistled or performed
naked in front of the tub, it stilled
itself. Afterward though, it was worse,
sloshing like a brew over the beveled
edges and into the dirt. The Exorcist's
dotter tried poetry and puppet show
and flash photography. She did a stum-
bling striptease out of a cassock, baked
it a cranberry tart. Later, she realized
what had spilt had found a way under
and into the groundwater. When they
came in their suits and smocks, pumps
and overalls, aprons and leather—when
they came in their microminis and
button-downs—when they came neatly
filed and in lockstep to the Exorcist's
home, for the Exorcist's dotter, their
teeth were dark with it, because they
were smiling.

knew a bit about second fiddle. Inside her second fiddle case, there was no need for a weapon like the mafia do it. So she carried a fiddle in her second fiddle case, a second fiddle, and with it took second chair in the children's symphony. There was only the one other, better child, who practiced more. The Protectorate's dotter had immense talent but was not driven to prove it. She was salutatorian of her high school class, and did not bother to win a Westinghouse, though she was very good at Westing. She was happy to maintain a low profile, and called herself, after the Rodin, "la femme accroupie," but again, she did not flash anyone. Crupy knew what was expected of her—a relaxed sense of her own royalty and that she not show herself to be "country." Maintaining the shift upward by looking bored, she was not to reach too high too quickly, not to ruffle by flying the skyfeathers nor step on by walking too uprightly the skytoes— the shiny toes. Instead, she should marry well. Expectations were limited to this, and it was easily accomplished, what with some good books, bought secondhand, to sleep inside, and a

series of lovers, all aspiring revolu-
tionaries with a love of guns, guns and
Vivaldi, who strove for her.

had a penchant for nuts: almond, pistachio, macadamia, walnut, acorn. She found herself abnormal and reveled in the finding, studying every last scrap on the properties and attitudes of such. She learned to recognize abnormal's most salient features, specifically, a certain telltale thickness of the bangs. One day, because she knew what to look for, she met another just like her. Naturally, they had a contest—who could be most damaged. It was more complicated than that, however. You see, physical is only surface, of this the two were well aware—the mind-body split was in fact a favorite. It was one of a number of splits they shared, including a banana at Dairy Queen because, despite being brutally pitted, they were their only friends. The problem came when the Bird-Filled-Up dotter wanted nuts—to feed her inner birds. The other dotter's inside species were highly allergic. She shouldn't have even been in the Dairy Queen. They compromised. The Bird-Filled-Up dotter got her nuts. And the other dotter got more damage. So much, so profound, that it went soul.

is not. Biology plays a bit part, being shit.

Shit, you may have heard, is of the body and must be embraced. Wrapped in cloaks of feces, the lovers of excess understand by what foul logic the child must be removed, cleaned, and offered up to the expense-paying proxies. (Because the Surrogate, having no inner resources, must hate the squalling thing.)

Unlike those educated in the finer shitpoints, the Surrogate admits hatred into the building (usually a hospital). The proxies, on the other hand, do not have to ride a shitwagon into the whiteworld or through it. Just, they must have the education and also money.

In certain countries adoption may not occur without the channeling of funds. These certain countries are all of the countries.

The dotter of the Surrogate must be given the proper foundation on which to be built or grown. Sometimes, average national incomes are considered, weighed against or with sexual preference, antidepressants, possible facial deformation, politics.

Money is shit: this has been demonstrated.

It is said that any stench can become bearable, a commonplace. But every day does not equal survivable. That is why death is every day: the kinder kind, murder; the variant suicides; the cancers; starvation; allegory; and the giving up of whole pounds of the self—eight, nine, even twelve—to strangers.

had wanted them to name her, but they refused, nearly non-secular in their fervor against. Each had a specific design in which she was to become critical. A name would be limiting, inconvenient, confusing, identity condoning. The labcoat needed a model system. The eyepatch needed an eye, the tweed—a twitterer. The luddites could have thrived with continued dictation, they felt. A head wished to become a chair, at the very least retain the futures of several distressed factota. An emeritus thumb wrestled with one of several ideas of death, which had been biding time in shiny shiny scars since the third degree. So the dotter did not receive a name nor a list of initials. She was offered a number, and told not to give it out to coeds who were constantly lunging from beneath stairwells. Her number, I have no problem telling you, was four. They affixed it to her face and her collar, to make her easily recognizable, although only to them, one or a few at a time, from across a dark bar or a quad. Nights, she scrubbed. She scrubbed and scrubbed and scrubbed. The number, upon close examination, appeared to be made of ticky-tacky, but each night came out all the same.

sat in a cool patch of light, requiring. Of what she required, she was unsure. It was always to look down, down between her legs to see stars. The fishbowl undid constellations as it moved through them, penetrating their dimensions, adding to them reflection. She thought perhaps others, but wasn't that nonsense when she had a universe? The Astronaut and the Astronaut's dotter spent hours sometimes, mapping. In documentation she found her solitary joy. Someday an other, beyond this bottle, would unroll the tight screws of paper. She knew of course when it would happen—after she was dust—a cloud of particles glassed in the ship that separated her and the Astronaut from naught. Eventually, she knew the two of them would find it necessary to turn inward. In earnest, they would begin to chart each other's skins, and she knew also the grief entailed would be unlike the grief imagined. Because there would be nothing, nothing for it.

5.

THIEF

Blessed be the fruit.

—Margaret Atwood

She rifled through the vasectomy papers. It wasn't there. An irre-vocability clause. She'd come to the lockbox unbeknownst. From the beginning she'd held onto the solar guarantee. She'd stapled it to her nipple—the least favorite, on the teabag breast. Days. She had been given days, and lit ones. But was she then barred from revolution, the inside of her own throat, its muscled slope? She would not hatch. But not ever? It had to be in the language, something she had missed agreeing to. A mention of the zeroed, the unconnected, the ganymedes, spurt and over. Someone had drawn these up. And hadn't foreskinned? Hadn't imagined her exclusion? How it would reckon her? She counted. Wound. She counted. Duel. She counted. Triage. Fear. Thief.

Among the infinite ballgown you lose the dotter. You were a snuck-in, tucked between meathooks and porchswings, and you picked one out. An arrowroot, a sweetstack. You tried her on by scrawling names in permanent ink. Foreheads, places of worship. She fit to you though you had been charged, static. She fit inside you, all the digits. You reconnoitered, waited for a slip to outchance her—a sateen gap in the links. One barb dropped, one slow fit of the pendulum and you would ascend with your porridge. But goldie was lock, lock, locked. Grr. Boom. Cotillion over. Flashlights out, campers. Honey down.

I stole her. In the cellar—one dotter, a snatched piece. You thought that meant more were. There were never more. I blame it on the croup. When you had a fit and flooded over the cinderblocks, I begged for you: woodenbowl, wunderbar, spoon, and/or razor. I was by the trains grounded, a well for spark. I was tuberous and eyeblind much like a dotter, but spat fire. I could pass. I always was passing—those weren't really children I had. I was un-exited from, except for buoys, but who counts buoys. I will. I will count them. Buoys you don't count have that wet wool smell. Yard, or navy. The dotter I caught under the earth was a contagion of starch and cotton. Gluten-love: she was better baked than boiled, with whitefish, on dark toast. That kind of dotter is like a grave. She won't ask flowers. Still. One feels better if one arranges them, her hair like a banquet, like a matchbox city. But I wouldn't know. I am not upfront with the progeny, do not sling, accessorize. Call my style mounded. I love the dirty ones left dirty. Fingers, fingers. Fingers on the baby.

: rules

1. A mutter can enter the dottery and leave the dottery with.

2. A mutterer cannot enter, or having entered, is weighed, and prohibited exit unless, and only unless, upon leaving the scales are exact.

3. Muttering then, can be reduced to a certain freedom through doorways combined with accepted levels of acquisition. To mutter is to engage in these limited capitalisms.

4. Only mutters mutter. A mutterer must refrain from muttering. This is what causes the telltale stammer, the self-edition, dieting.

5. On the inside, an odd dotter may grow sympathetic. She will feel for the mutterers come to windowshop—the ones who walk the dottery fingering with eyes. Wide-and-doe-and-hook-and.

6. The odd dotter may come to diet. Such events are conspiracies of air, and thus redundant.

7. Yet, if a mutterer can become weightless, and a dotter become weightless, the scales will be exact and something, in their favor, may tip.

Notice that the defining feature of a mutterer is her er. She is differentiated from the mutter she would be by her own defect. (All mutterers stammer, stutter, rehash and stab.)* To er is woman, to forklift—the knives. All she need do is amputate her flaw. Yet her mistake—her undesirable plenitude—cannot be removed because it is not there. Her fault is an echo of fault, and to excise an echo—do not take away, fill. But the dottery won't have her. She is not allowed to carry out. And her resulting blood, her attempts to truncate a nonexistent limb, will weaken her beyond tea taken sweet despite dangers. Sugar, dotters, is after all alcohol. Sugar is the singe beneath the carmine blouse, the charred rib, phantom mastectomy. Er is the room she has made for emergency—sirenless.

---

* Everyone should be capable, should envision herself a mutterer. (Murtherer.) Of dotters especially. The Amish know this. You are probably reading this because you are a poet or a mother, my mother, or some other blood relative, or because you are trying to prove your goatee soul patch tousled hair cock looks good on a feminist. It does. But this-here-this is my body not your five (count them) unpregnant unpuzzles of cadaver, and you and I are not a television.

You aren't mammarian. Can't have. What a dotter needs is the thin gruel you've vanquished from your good-for-nothings. We don't care how small you've grown. How raked the stage when you were a white factory. How you rolled from room to room as on a cart. What tubes. A dotter needs full blowns. What are you thinking— trusting in chemistry? The molecules will seer her from the inside, like glass. You must do what's natural, though pain sends you to dice her against a wall. Pain is natural. Pain is good. Good is natural. Voila. We knew the proof. We knew we knew it. Just as we know if you won't flooze, get blousy, well then, you've ruined her. Them all. That's why we mustn't let you get your hands on one. They aren't natural, your hands. They taste gray, like latex, even from a distance. Hoofish. Mannish. Mannequine. Not animal enough.

You think it is purely a matter of dipping into the coffers. It is not. What makes one transparental is the process's instability, its teetering ink. Forms. Pages filled only to be blown across the curb into oncoming traffic like blind acrobats. Tossed jetsam. Whole salad-flocks of forms. Cry fowl. What you can't stop believing is that you were one. That you ached and spat the way a dotter was made to. Coldly nubile, a crease inside a fold, a morsel, dropped punctuation, drumbitten, a nipped-in-the-bud. And that you won't have. It's the refusal. The eternal matricycle not turning over. The snake disgorging its rattle. Skins will shed until no skins are left, and a dotter is all skin. The stuck will hop. Bier, bier.

: application to mutter

What are your salient qualities?
Lacking anything oceanic, what have you to offer?
Name your five fastest bed-dives.
Swan? Nose? Boxing?
When a dotter cries out in the night for a balm to be applied—
should you experience that as crisis or candy?
Whose books have you authored?
If you became capable of cloning or of budding which would you defer?
Are you in this for the long hallway or the eventual draperies?
If a stipulation were to keep the dotter outdoors, could you withstand
nature?
Explain your want in fewer than eighteen letters disregarding d, h, and a.
Disregarding a, r, and a.
During the period when your dotter doesn't love you anymore, you will
need a maintenance strategy.
Please develop it in another darkroom, on a more compelling crucifix.

There was a dotter in the spring. Wound there, coiled to strike. She circled back and forth the picket. She said she wouldn't work. "I wouldn't work," she said, "not for you." She was right about the too many reactions, allergies she might have. Pine dust, azaleas, mites. That someone would move or vacuum just to have her was foreign. People pay money but people don't clean or stop swearing. People give up caffeine and alcohol and the gym but rarely cigarettes. She stayed in the spring inside the couch inside the lounge inside the dottery. Not exactly waiting, but not watching the television either. Outside, the reasons she breathed that way would be trickier to identify. Mold may kill, but its familiar dapple on bread and in damp cabinets is a signal for bleach. In the dottery, strategies had been approved and implemented. Who gives a sure thing up for weather? Her ribcage was a double boiler, an aquarium. She kept her lungs there. Pets.

Mornings, dotters re-skin themselves. They tiptoe into their parachutes for world ascent. All dotters, jumpers, and head first. They move through their skin, about them in its great diaphanies, to the center where the soles are. Almost every day the skins lick up in great petals to seal each dotter in her velum. Only at night do dotters undo their inner vestment. For cleaning. For cleaning and storage. They peel, like hose, the skin for laying into large skin baskets. They fit themselves into silhouette, the puddled dreamblood they've produced in side effect. If, at dawn, a dotter's skin will not rejoin her, that day is a meditation day. She will mull her twin failures: to lace and to congeal. Such dotters prove immobile, fervent not to stain. For this, we should be grateful. A loose dotter, unbound by that organ's narcotic meshwork—by the shame of its distinction—she would always be in danger of incorporating.

When you bellylow a dotter, she does not drive herself out into the forest with torches, or seal her preserves. She stares blinkless like a dolly. The unblinking kind. Bellylows were meant, I know, to bring on the gloaming—but a dotter resists betweens, being one. Yes. She has long been a fellow since you saw your father's own and drummed up a replacement. (Ah, theory, a pillow of down-over-the-face in times of reckless, of atrocity.) But this is night and day, not the other two. Still, you croon and croon and she cannot grow more rigid. You corpse-cradle her. How comforting to hold something that does not wriggle or pivot. Something that fixes itself for hurdy-gurdying. As if neutered. She has always done this, and she has done this not for you or I, and not only not-to-dream, but in feckless imitation of a beloved.

Dear one for me

Out, out against the lying of the knight.
Chivalry is cuckoo and wrong.

                              Spam, dot

*

Dear one for me,

Your breasts have been so tender. What I know I am going to love
about you is your mouth. It will be red and dark with many teeth. It
may be that your mouth has been astonished into an O. Otherwise,
it is a slit, lips luxury you borrow from a pencil. I know you are not
involved with the law. I know you will be on my side and that I am to
have an Annie Oakley hat and a shiny gun you will think better of
but give me anyway. That is down for my sixth birthday. The ledger
does not tell the color of your hair, although I imagine it changes the
way shoes change and lovers. I know you will be so honest, until I
hate you, and that then you will learn to lie a little—butter at room
temperature. Before I come to you, your life is a seventy-city tour.
Then it will be a house with sad music, then an arboretum, finally
rain. On the morning you find out about me, by pissing, the world
will either seem very large and beautiful, or it will be as if all the
cards have hearted, spayed, and clubbed you. You must try not to
forget.

                              The diamonds, Dot

Dear one for me,

Call. At this point that would mean a hose connected from mouth to mouth. I'm not on the inside, you just look for me there. What I want to say is, get better. How do you think you will be able to float me without weight? A lampoil layer of joy? Also, listen to your sister. She has never regretted you. Your foot is only a pedal—do not neglect the other strengths. Wheels. A sapling core. Train yourself to bend again, the kind of bending that might require water. Broken, light will not answer the phone. And you haven't a machine. I will someday, if found, show you how to build a machine.

And more throats, Dot

*

Dear one,

It is undeniably true. Bling. Dotters have been known to be seduced by candy, shiny red fastnesses, by the promise that their navel is actually a powerful weapon. These dotters are lately the favorites.

Take me anyway, Dot

I shall tell you now, though you can't believe it, the story of the dottery. Before you are born, there is a line of us waiting for you. And there is a line of you, waiting too. We stand very straight. Tall, and—also—queued quite smartly. We blaze, we are pumped. It is very important, we know, though none of us know how we know, that there be no wavering, no looking past the next. We are like the teeth on a gear, orderly like that, though if there is circularity involved on another plane, as there is in gears, we are not aware. Some who would like to stand in line are not allowed. A velvet rope. Those some keep looking at us, we who would not admit we're thieves. And there are others, who do not come near, with eyes that say The Hell, and some who do not look. I want to make this perfectly clear: not everyone wants. Many of you will be thrown past our line into a crowd of those who do not. You are to be wolved. Still, some of the lone may learn to want you, though some never. Dot, listen. A great number of you will carry the large open howl given you by those who preferred not to. And the rest, you will crave silent and ashamedly the moon, as—before you—do we.

It is later. It is all too much.

I face my dotter, the one I should never have taken. An icestorm has lain waste to our hair. Her solemnity, which had been a braid, is snapped in half. Pine tree. "What have you been doing?" I ask her. She has a heart for a face. She has a heart where her mouth should be, a heart at the crux of her left elbow, little hearts in her fingers, between her legs—a heart. She models them. "I have been working on development," she says. I wonder at her, "Cellular?" "No," as she has debunked all my theories, she denies me biology. "Ulular." She is teaching herself and others how to bay without moon. She thinks it is her vocation—the frequent disruption of brick: serial, howling windows. Looking as liberty. I know better. She is still, very still in the basement, and she is not aware. I forego revelation, mesmerized. O, her blood. We table—share a cup of firemilk. She sips, and the beating of her face makes it a pink almost warm. I stare at the life. When it is time to go I offer my hand. She wraps it in a napkin, tucks it into her pocket. I have seen her do this many times before—with a half-eaten sparrow.

ACKNOWLEDGMENTS

Sections of this manuscript have been published in the following journals:

American Letters & Commentary, Coconut, Columbia Poetry Review, CutBank, Denver Quarterly, Free Verse, Ixnay Reader, Jubilat, LIT, No Tell Motel, Otoliths, Sentence, and *Typo.*